We are **The Moving Press**, an independent publishing company who love creating books for children. We are passionate about children's education and we believe that children learn best through play and interaction with others.

We created this book so your child can have fun learning interesting animal facts. Whether they repeat what they have learned to teachers, friends or family, every fact is an opportunity to learn something new and socialise.

We care greatly about the accuracy of our content. If you notice anything outdated or inaccurate in this book, please email us at **themovingpress@gmail.com**, and we will fix this immediately. We would also love to hear any general questions that you have for the author. If you enjoy this book, **please leave a review** for us. Every small comment helps.

Enjoy!

FANTASTIC FACTS

ANIMAL EDITION

AN A-Z
FOR CURIOUS KIDS

Hi there, wild ones! Are you ready for a whirlwind of crazy animal facts?

This book is for all animal enthusiasts. From A to Z you will discover facts about all of the weird and wonderful creatures that roam the Earth with us.

Whether you love amazing alligators or cuddly koalas, you're bound to learn something new in this book.

Look out for curious croc along the way - he has some questions for you!

Alligator

Alligators are one of the largest reptiles in the world and can grow up to 15 feet (4.5 metres) long. That's longer than a school bus!

Alligators are excellent swimmers and can swim up to 20 miles per hour in short bursts.

Alligators have an average lifespan of around 35-50 years in the wild.

Ant

Ants are really strong. They can carry objects that weigh up to 50 times their own body weight. That's like a human carrying a car!

Ants are found on every continent except Antarctica. There are over 12,000 species of ants, and they come in a wide variety of sizes, colors, and shapes.

Ants live in large groups called colonies. Each ant has a specific job, such as foraging for food, caring for young, or defending the colony.

Anglerfish

Anglerfish are named after the long fishing rod-like appendage on their head that has a glowing bulb on the end. This is used to attract prey towards their sharp teeth.

Anglerfish are deep-sea creatures that live in the dark depths of the ocean. Some live up to 4,500 meters deep.

Male Angler fish are much smaller than females. There are over 200 species of Anglerfish.

Anteater

Anteaters have tongues that can extend up to 2 feet (60 cm) long, which they use to catch ants and termites.

Anteaters have strong claws and are able to climb trees to access ant and termite nests. They are also strong swimmers..

Unlike most mammals, anteaters don't have any teeth. Instead, they use their long tongues to scoop up and swallow their food whole.

Anaconda

Anacondas are excellent swimmers. They can stay underwater for up to 10 minutes at a time!

Anacondas are not venomous, but they are still very dangerous. They use their strong muscles to constrict their prey and squeeze the life out of it.

Anacondas can eat very large meals. They have been known to eat animals such as deer, pigs, and even jaguars!

Armadillo

Armadillos are the only mammals that have bony armour. Their armour is made up of plates that cover the top, sides, back, and tail of their body.

Armadillos are nocturnal animals, which means they are most active at night. During the day, they sleep in their burrows to avoid the hot sun.

Armadillos have poor eyesight, but a great sense of smell which is used to locate food. They eat insects, fruit and small animals like lizards and snakes.

Can you remember?

On which continent will you <u>not</u> find any ants?

<u>Answer</u>

Antarctica

Bear

There are 8 species of bears in the world. They can be found on every continent except Australia and Antarctica. The most common species are the polar bear, the brown bear, and the black bear.

Bears have an excellent sense of smell! They can smell food from miles away.

Bears hibernate during the winter months. They build dens and sleep for several months without eating or drinking.

Bat

Bats are very important for our ecosystem. They eat insects, including mosquitoes and other pests that can harm crops.

There are over 1,300 species of bats. The smallest is the bumblebee bat, which is about the size of a bee. The largest, the flying fox, has a wingspan of up to 6 feet (1.8 metres)

Bats use echolocation to find their way around in the dark. They emit high-pitched sounds and listen for the echoes to determine the location and distance of objects.

Badger

Badgers have black and white stripes on their faces, which help them to recognise each other. No two badgers have the exact same stripes!

Badgers are excellent diggers and can dig tunnels up to 10 metres long in just one night!

Badgers are nocturnal animals, which means they are most active at night. During the day, they like to sleep in their cosy burrows.

Bee

Bees are important pollinators that help flowers and plants grow. Without bees, we wouldn't have many of the fruits and vegetables we love to eat!

Bees can fly up to 15 miles per hour, making them one of the fastest insects in the world.

Bees live in hives with thousands of other bees. They work together to keep the hive clean and to collect nectar and pollen from flowers.

Beaver

Beavers are incredible
engineers! They build dams
and lodges using branches,
mud, and stones. These
structures can be as tall
as 6 feet (1.8 metres).

Beavers are herbivores,
which means they only
eat plants. They love
to eat the bark from
trees and water plants.

Beavers are able to swim
underwater. They can
close their ears and nose
to keep water out, and
they have clear eyelids
that act like goggles.

Butterfly

There are thousands of species of butterflies around the world, each with its own unique patterns and colours.

Butterflies go through a transformation process called metamorphosis. They start out as eggs, hatch into caterpillars, and then form a cocoon before emerging as a beautiful butterfly!

Butterflies have a special way of tasting food. They have taste receptors on their feet and use them to taste the nectar of flowers before they land on them.

Can you remember?

Is it <u>true</u> or <u>false</u> that badgers are great diggers?

<u>Answer</u>
It's true

Camel

Camels are adapted to life in the desert. They have thick fur to protect them from the sun and can go for long periods without water.

Camels have three stomachs. This allows them to eat tough, thorny plants and break them down into nutrients.

Camels have two sets of eyelashes and can close their nostrils to protect themselves from blowing sand.

Cheetah

Cheetahs are the fastest land animals! They can run up to speeds of 70 miles per hour in short bursts to catch their prey.

Cheetahs have unique spots on their fur, which help them camouflage in the grasslands where they live.

Cheetahs have distinctive black tear marks on their faces that help protect their eyes from the sun and also help them see long distances.

Capybara

Capybaras are the largest rodents in the world. They can weigh as much as a grown-up person!

Capybaras love to swim and can stay underwater for up to 5 minutes. They have webbed feet that help them paddle through the water.

Capybaras are herbivores, which means they only eat plants. They like to munch on grass, aquatic plants, and fruits.

Crab

Crabs are crustaceans, which means they have a hard outer shell or 'exoskeleton' to protect their soft bodies.

Crabs have 5 pairs of legs, with the first pair of legs being modified into claws or pincers called chelae, which they use for defense, hunting, and gathering food.

There are over 4,500 species of crabs, ranging in size from tiny pea crabs to giant Japanese spider crabs that can span up to 12 feet (3.7 metres).

Clownfish

Clownfish are small, brightly coloured fish that are found in warm ocean waters around the world.

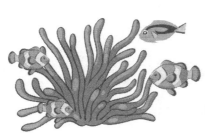

Clownfish are the only known fish that are able to live among the stinging tentacles of sea anemones without being harmed.

Clownfish are named for their distinctive colouration, which includes bright orange, red, and black stripes.

Can you remember?

How many stomachs
does a camel have?

Answer

3 Stomachs

Dolphin

Dolphins have a streamlined body shape that allows them to swim at high speeds. Some species can reach speeds of up to 37 miles per hour (60 km/h).

There are over 40 species of dolphins, ranging in size from about 3 feet to over 30 feet in length (1-9 metres).

Dolphins are known for their playful behaviour and can often be seen leaping out of the water, riding waves, and playing with objects like seaweed or balls.

Deer

Deer are known for their distinctive antlers, which are grown and shed annually by males of most species.

Deer have keen senses, including excellent hearing and a sense of smell that is a thousand times more sensitive than a human's.

Deer are herbivores and feed on a variety of plants, including leaves, twigs, fruits, and grasses.

23

Dragonfly

Dragonflies are found all over the world, and there are more than 5,000 species of dragonflies known to science.

Although dragonflies have 6 legs they cannot walk!

Dragonflies have excellent vision and are able to see in all directions at once due to their large compound eyes.

Donkey

Donkeys are known for their incredible strength and are able to carry heavy loads over long distances.

Donkeys have a lifespan of up to 50 years, which is longer than the average lifespan of many other domesticated animals.

Donkeys have a strong memory and are able to recognise familiar people and animals, even after long periods of time.

Duck

Ducks are sociable animals and are often found in groups called 'paddlings'. This also protects them from predators.

A duck's quack doesn't echo, and nobody knows why!

The shape of ducks' eyes means they can see things close and far away in sharp focus. They can also see 340 degrees around because of the position of their eyes.

Can you remember?

How many legs does a dragonfly have?

Answer
6 legs

Elephant

Elephants are the largest land animals in the world, with males weighing up to 6000 kilograms (14,000 pounds) and standing over 10 feet (3 metres) tall.

Elephants have a long trunk, which they use to breathe, smell, drink, and grasp objects like food and tree branches.

Elephants have thick skin that protects them from the sun and insect bites, and they often cover themselves in mud and dirt to keep cool.

Eagle

Eagles are birds of prey that are known for their sharp talons, hooked beaks, and excellent eyesight.

Eagles are powerful fliers and can soar for hours without flapping their wings because of their large wingspan and aerodynamic design.

Eagles are carnivores and eat a variety of prey, including fish, small mammals, birds, and reptiles.

Eel

Eels have long, snake-like bodies and are typically brown, green, or black in colour.

Eels are a type of fish that are found in both freshwater and saltwater habitats around the world.

Some species of eels can live for up to 80 years, making them one of the longest-lived species of fish.

Emu

Emus are large, flightless birds that are native to Australia. They are covered in soft fluffy feathers.

Emus are the second-largest living bird species in the world, after the ostrich. They can grow up to 2 metres tall.

Emus have strong legs and can run up to speeds of 30 miles per hour (50 kilometres per hour).

Elk

Elk, also known as wapiti, are one of the largest species of deer. They are found in North America and parts of Asia.

Elk have distinctive antlers that can grow up to 4 feet (1.2 metres) long.

Elk can run up to 40 miles per hour (64 km per hour) meaning they could beat horses in short races.

Can you remember?

Are eagles carnivores or herbivores?

Fox

Foxes are known for their distinctive bushy tails which they use for balance, warmth and communicating with each other.

Foxes are nocturnal animals, which means they are most active at night.

There are over 30 different species of foxes, and they are found all over the world, except for Antarctica.

Flamingo

Flamingoes are born with grey feathers, but their feathers turn pink over time due to the food that they eat.

There are 6 different species of flamingoes, and they are found in parts of Africa, South America, Central America, and the Caribbean.

Flamingoes can sleep while standing on one leg, and will often tuck their heads under their wings to conserve body heat.

Frog

Frogs undergo a metamorphosis from a tadpole, which has gills and lives in water, to an adult frog, which has lungs and lives on land.

Frogs are amphibians, which means they can live both in water and on land.

Frogs come in many different colours and sizes, and there are over 7,000 species of frogs in the world. Some are poisonous!

Falcon

Falcons are known for their incredible speed and agility in flight. The peregrine falcon is the fastest of all birds.

Falcons have excellent eyesight, which allows them to spot prey from high in the sky.

Falcons are trained by humans for hunting and falconry, which is an old-fashioned practice that dates back thousands of years.

Ferret

Ferrets have been domesticated for over 2,500 years and were originally bred for hunting rodents.

Ferrets are very flexible and can fit through small spaces, which makes them good escape artists.

Ferrets are able to sleep for up to 18 hours a day, but when they are awake, they are very active and playful.

Can you remember?

How many hours per day can a ferret sleep for?

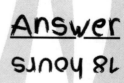

Answer
18 hours

Giraffe

Giraffes are the tallest mammals in the world, with their long necks reaching up to 6 feet (1.8 metres) in length.

Giraffes can run up to 35 miles per hour, which makes them one of the fastest land animals.

Giraffes have excellent eyesight and can see over long distances, which helps them detect predators.

Gorilla

Gorillas are intelligent animals with problem-solving abilities. They actually have a close genetic relationship to humans, with a DNA similarity of around 98%.

Gorillas are the largest primates in the world and can weigh up to 180 kilograms (400 pounds).

Gorillas have a dominant male called a silverback who leads the troop and is responsible for protecting the group.

Gecko

Geckos are a type of lizard known for their sticky feet, which allow them to climb on walls and ceilings.

Some geckos are able to change colour to blend in with their surroundings, which helps them avoid predators.

Geckos have a third eye called a parietal eye on the top of their head. It helps them sense light and dark.

Goat

Goats have a unique digestive system that allows them to eat almost anything, including plants that are poisonous to other animals.

Goats are very agile and are excellent climbers. They can climb steep cliffs and trees.

Goats have rectangular shaped pupils that give them a wide field of vision and excellent depth perception.

Gopher

Gophers are burrowing rodents that *live in* underground tunnels and are found throughout North America.

Gophers have large front teeth that are perfect for gnawing on roots and tubers, their primary food source.

Gophers are known for their extensive tunnel systems, which can span up to 2,000 square feet (186 square metres).

Can you remember?

What is the tallest mammal?

Answer
A giraffe

Hippo

Hippos are the third-largest land animal, after elephants and rhinos.

Hippos have a lifespan of around 40-50 years in the wild.

Despite their large size, hippos can run up to 19 miles per hour on land and swim up to 30 miles per hour in water. They can hold their breath for up to 5 minutes.

Hedgehog

Hedgehogs are nocturnal animals, which means they are most active at night.

Hedgehogs will roll into a tight ball when they feel threatened, protecting themselves with their sharp spines.

Hedgehogs have poor eyesight but an excellent sense of smell and hearing.

Hummingbird

Hummingbirds are tiny birds that are only a few inches long and weigh less than a penny. They can hover in mid-air by quickly flapping their wings.

Hummingbirds are the only birds that can fly backwards. They can also fly upside down!

Hummingbirds have long, thin beaks that they use to sip nectar from flowers.

Hare

Hares are much larger than rabbits and have longer ears and legs.

Hares are known for their incredible speed and agility. They can reach speeds of up to 45 miles per hour.

Hares have a unique behaviour called "boxing" where they stand on their hind legs and hit each other with their front paws during the breeding season.

Horse

Horses have excellent senses including sight, hearing, and smell. Their eyes are located on the sides of their head, which gives them almost 360-degree vision.

You can tell the age of a horse by the length of its teeth.

Horses can sleep standing up and have a special locking mechanism in their legs that allows them to do so.

Can you remember?

What is a hippo's lifespan in the wild?

<u>Answer</u>
40 - 50 years

Ibex

Ibex are a type of wild mountain goat found in Europe, Asia and Africa. They are well adapted to living in rocky, mountainous terrain.

Ibex are known for their impressive horns, which can grow up to several feet long. Both male and female ibex have horns, but the males' horns are usually larger.

Ibex are herbivores and primarily eat grasses, leaves, and other vegetation.

Ibis

The ibis is a long-legged wading bird with a long, curved bill.

The most well-known species of ibis is probably the sacred ibis, which was worshipped by the ancient Egyptians and depicted in many of their artworks.

Ibis have a unique feeding behaviour where they use their long bill to probe into the mud and water to find small fish, insects, and other prey.

Iguana

Iguanas are large, herbivorous lizards that are native to the tropics of Central and South America, as well as some islands in the Caribbean.

They are known for their ability to change colour, depending on their mood and environment.

Iguanas are able to detach and regrow their tails *if they feel* threatened or are attacked by a predator.

Impala

Impalas are medium-sized antelopes that are found in eastern and southern Africa.

They are known for their remarkable jumping ability, and can leap up to 10 feet (3 metres) high and 30 feet (9 metres) in length.

Male impalas have long, curved horns that they use for fighting during mating season.

Can you remember?

Are male or female Ibex horns longer?

<u>Answer</u>
Male

Jellyfish

There are over 2,000 different species of jellyfish. Some species are as small as a pinhead, while others can grow up to 8 feet (2.4 metres) in diameter.

Jellyfish have no brain, heart, or bones. Instead, they have a simple nervous system that allows them to sense their surroundings and respond to stimuli.

Jellyfish are found in every ocean in the world, from the surface waters to the deep sea. Some species are even capable of surviving in freshwater.

Jaguar

Jaguars are the largest cats in the Americas and the third-largest cats in the world, after tigers and lions.

They stalk and ambush their prey rather than chasing it down and they often use their camouflage to blend in with their surroundings before attacking.

Jaguars are excellent swimmers and are known to hunt fish and caimans in the water.

Jackals

Jackals are medium-sized canids that belong to the same family as wolves, coyotes, and dogs.

There are three species of jackals: the golden jackal, the black-backed jackal, and the side-striped jackal.

Jackals are omnivores, which means they eat both animals and plants. Their diet includes small mammals, birds, insects and fruits.

Can you remember?

In which oceans can you find jellyfish?

Kangaroo

Kangaroos are able to jump long distances by using their powerful hind legs but cannot jump backwards.

The red kangaroo is the largest marsupial in the world, with adult males standing up to 6 feet (1.8 metres) tall and weighing up to 91 kilograms (200 pounds).

Female kangaroos have a pouch on their belly where they carry and nurse their young, called joeys.

Koala

Koalas sleep for up to 20 hours a day. They are most active at night and during the early morning hours.

Koalas are known for their remarkable jumping ability, and can leap up to 10 feet (3 metres) high and 30 feet (9 metres) in length.

Koalas have a unique set of fingerprints that are very similar to human fingerprints. This has been helpful in studying and tracking individual koalas in the wild.

Kookaburra

The kookaburra is a bird species that is native to Australia and New Guinea. The most well-known is the laughing kookaburra.

The laughing kookaburra is known for its distinctive call, which sounds like a loud, echoing laugh.

Kookaburras have a unique hunting strategy. They will often perch in a tree and wait for prey to pass below, before swooping down to catch it.

Komodo Dragon

Komodo dragons are the world's largest lizards, growing up to 10 feet (3 metres) in length and weighing up to 150 kilograms (330 pounds).

They have a forked tongue that helps them to pick up scents in the air, which they use to locate prey.

The Komodo dragon is the national animal of Indonesia, and they are a popular tourist attraction on the islands where they live.

Kiwi

The kiwi is a flightless bird that is native to New Zealand. It is also the national symbol of New Zealand.

Kiwis are unique among birds because they have nostrils at the end of their long, curved beaks. This helps them to locate insects and other small prey underground.

Kiwis have very strong legs and can run quickly, even over rough terrain. They use their wings to balance and change direction when running.

Can you remember?

How long can a koala sleep for?

<u>Answer</u>
Up to 20 hours

Lion

Lions are apex predators, meaning they are at the top of the food chain. They hunt medium to large sized wildebeest, zebra, and buffalo.

Lionesses are the primary hunters in the pride, while male lions defend the territory and the pride from intruders.

Lions have a powerful roar that can be heard up to 5 miles away. They use this roar to communicate with other lions and to announce their presence to potential rivals.

Llama

Llamas are native to the Andes Mountains in South America, where they have been used as pack animals and sources of wool and meat for thousands of years.

Llamas have three stomach compartments, which help them digest their food efficiently.

Llamas have a lifespan of around 20-25 years and can grow up to 6 feet (1.8 metres) tall and weigh up to 180 kilograms (400 pounds)

Ladybug

Ladybugs, also known as ladybirds or lady beetles, are small beetles. There are over 5,000 species of ladybugs worldwide.

Ladybugs are typically red or orange with black spots, but can also be yellow or brown with white or black spots.

The smallest ladybug is only about 1 millimetre in length, while the largest can be up to 1 inch (25 mm). They can fly as fast as 37 miles per hour.

Lobster

Lobsters have 5 pairs of legs, with the front pair of legs adapted into large claws that are used for defense and catching prey.

Lobsters are capable of regenerating lost limbs, and can even regrow their claws if they are removed.

Lobsters have been known to live for over 100 years in the wild, and are thought to be one of the longest-lived species of arthropod.

Leopard

Leopards' spots are called "rosettes" because they look like the petals of a rose. Their fur helps them blend in with their surroundings.

Leopards are amazing climbers and can haul their prey up into trees to keep it safe from other predators.

Leopards are very fast runners and can reach speeds of up to 35 miles per hour. They are also very strong and can carry prey that is up to three times their own weight.

71

Can you remember?

How far away can a lion's roar be heard?

<u>Answer</u>
Up to 5 miles

Monkey

There are over 260 species of monkeys, ranging from the tiny pygmy marmoset, which weighs around 100 grams (4 ounces), to the mandrill, which can weigh up to 54 kilograms (120 pounds).

Some monkeys, such as the howler monkey, have a very loud call that can be heard up to 3 miles away.

Some monkeys have opposable thumbs, which allow them to hold objects. This is similar to human hands. In fact, humans share about 98% of their DNA with chimpanzees.

Moose

Moose are the largest species of deer and can weigh up to 800 kg (1,800 pounds). Male moose (bulls) have antlers that can span up to 6 feet (1.8 metres) across. They shed and regrow their antlers each year.

Moose are found in North America, Europe, and Asia, and are well adapted to life in cold, snowy climates.

They are excellent swimmers and can dive to depths of up to 20 feet (6 metres), swim at 6 miles per hour and stay underwater for up to 30 seconds.

Manta

Mantas are some of the largest fish in the ocean, with some reaching up to 23 feet (7 metres) in wingspan. They are related to sharks not stingrays.

Mantas do not have a stinger in their tail and are not considered dangerous to humans. They may approach divers and interact with them in a friendly manner.

Mantas are found in warm, tropical waters around the world, including in the Atlantic, Indian, and Pacific oceans. They have a lifespan of up to 50 years.

Mongoose

Many species of mongoose have long, sleek bodies and short legs, which allow them to move quickly and easily through dense vegetation.

Mongooses are known for their acrobatic ability and can climb trees, swim, and even stand on their hind legs to get a better view of their surroundings.

There are about 40 different species of mongoose. The Indian grey mongoose are known for their ability to kill venomous snakes.

Mouse

Mice have compact bodies with a pointed snout, small ears, and a long, scaly tail. They have a great sense of smell and use their whiskers to help navigate through their environment.

Mice are known for their quick reflexes and agility, which help them escape from predators and navigate through small spaces.

Mice have been used extensively in scientific research and have contributed to numerous breakthroughs in the fields of genetics, neuroscience, and medicine.

Can you remember?

which animal can grow
antlers up to 6 feet?

Narwhal

Narwhals are a type of whale that *live in the* Arctic waters around Canada, Greenland, and Russia. They are known for their long, spiral tusks that can grow up to 10 feet (3 metres) long.

Narwhals use their tusks to break through the *ice* to breathe, hunt for food, and to attract mates.

They are excellent divers and can *dive* to depths of over a mile in search of food.

Newt

Newts are small, semi-aquatic salamanders that *live in freshwater* habitats around the world. They spend part of their *life cycle in water* and part on land.

Newts have the ability to regenerate their limbs, tail, spinal cord, heart, and *even parts of their brain if they become damaged or lost.*

Newts have a unique adaptation that allows them to breathe through their skin. They absorb oxygen directly from the water, helping them breathe underwater.

Numbat

Numbats are small marsupials that are native to Western Australia. They are very similar to anteaters.

Numbats have distinctive markings on their back that resemble stripes, which help to camouflage them in their habitat.

Numbats are able to eat up to 20,000 termites in a single day, which helps to control termite populations in their habitat.

Nudibranch

Nudibranchs are a type of sea slug that are found in oceans worldwide. They come in many bright colours and intricate patterns.

Nudibranchs have a reputation for being toxic or poisonous, which helps to deter predators from eating them.

Nudibranchs have a very important job in the ocean ecosystem. They help to keep the ocean clean by eating things like algae and small animals.

Can you remember?

Do newts live on land or in the water?

Answer
They live in both

Owl

Owls are nocturnal birds of prey, which means they hunt and eat other animals. They are known for their silent flight, sharp talons, and powerful beaks.

Their eyes are so big that they cannot move them in their sockets, but they can swivel their heads up to 270 degrees.

There are over 200 species of owls. The smallest owl, the elf owl, is only about 5 inches tall, while the largest owl, the Eurasian eagle-owl, can be over 2 feet (0.6 metres) tall.

Octopus

An octopus has blue blood, 3 hearts and 9 brains. The largest octopus species is the giant Pacific octopus, which can grow up to 16 feet (4.9 metres).

Octopuses have the ability to change colour to blend in with their surroundings, making them masters of camouflage. They can also shoot ink clouds to confuse predators.

Octopuses are very intelligent and have been known to solve complex problems, navigate mazes, and even open jars to get food. They also don't have skeletons!

Otter

There are 13 different species of Otters. They are excellent swimmers and can hold their breath for up to 8 minutes underwater.

Otters are social animals that live in family groups called rafts. Sea otters hold hands while they sleep so they don't drift apart.

Otters have a thick coat of fur that helps to keep them warm in cold water. Sea otters have the thickest fur of any mammal, with up to one million hairs per square inch.

Ostrich

Ostriches cannot fly, but their wings are not useless. They use them for balance and to help them steer while running.

Ostriches are the fastest running birds and can sprint up to 43 miles per hour. They have powerful legs that can deliver lethal kicks to predators.

Ostriches can grow up to 9 feet (2.7 metres) tall and weigh over 140 kg (300 pounds), making them the largest birds in the world.

Can you remember?

How many hearts does an octopus have?

Puffin

Puffins are birds that have bright orange beaks and feet. They are also known as "clowns of the sea" because of their colorful appearance and playful behaviour.

Baby puffins are called "pufflings" and they are born with grey feathers. They stay in their nests for about 6 weeks before they are able to fly.

Puffins have special grooves on the roofs of their mouths that allow them to grip multiple fish while they catch more.

Panda

Giant pandas are native to China and are considered a national treasure. All giant pandas in zoos around the world are borrowed from China.

Despite being classified as a carnivore, pandas are herbivores and their diet consists mainly of bamboo. They spend over 12 hours a day eating up to 18 kg (40 pounds) of bamboo.

The black and white markings of pandas serve as a natural camouflage in their bamboo forest habitat, making them difficult to spot by predators.

90

Platypus

The duck-billed platypus is a unique and fascinating animal that is native to Australia.

It is semi-aquatic and spends much of its time in the water, using its webbed feet and powerful tail to swim and dive.

It is a monotreme, which means that it is one of the only mammals that lays eggs instead of giving birth to live young.

Penguin

Penguins are flightless birds that are highly adapted to *life in the water*. They are excellent swimmers and divers, and can hold their breath for up to 20 minutes.

Penguins are very social animals and like to huddle together for warmth. In fact, some penguin colonies can have over 1,000 penguins in them!

Penguins can be many different sizes. The little blue penguin is only about 16 inches tall, while the emperor penguin can be over 3 feet (0.9 metres) tall.

Porcupine

Porcupines are covered in sharp quills that help protect them from predators. Baby porcupines are born with soft quills that harden within a few days.

Porcupines are great climbers and can use their sharp claws to climb trees and rocky cliffs to escape danger.

Porcupines have poor eyesight, but they have an excellent sense of smell and can locate food and predators using their noses.

Can you remember?

What is a baby puffin called?

<u>Answer</u>

A puffling

Quokkas

Quokkas are small marsupials that are native to Western Australia. They are often called the "world's happiest animal" because they seem to be constantly smiling!

Quokkas are about the size of a domestic cat and can jump up to three times their own body length!

Quokkas are nocturnal animals that are part of the kangaroo family. they like to hop around and carry their offspring in a front pouch

Quail

Quails are small birds that belong to the pheasant family. There are over 130 different species, ranging from just a few inches to over a foot long.

Quails are highly social birds and are often found in groups, known as coveys. They are fast runners and can reach speeds of 15mph.

Quails have a unique defense mechanism - when threatened, they will burst into flight with a sudden, explosive takeoff, which can startle predators and give the quail a chance to escape.

Quetzal

Quetzals are brightly coloured birds that are found in the rainforests of Central and South America.

The Resplendent Quetzal is the national bird of Guatemala and is considered one of the most beautiful birds in the world.

Quetzals are known for their long, trailing tail feathers, which can be over 3 feet (1 metres) long and are used during courtship displays.

Can you remember?

why are quokkas considered the happiest animals?

Answer

They always smile

Rabbit

Rabbits have two sets of incisor teeth that never stop growing, so they need to chew on things constantly to wear them down.

Just like deer, a female rabbit is called a doe and a male rabbit is called a buck. A baby rabbit is called a kit.

Rabbits have a field of vision that spans nearly 360 degrees, which means they can see behind them without even turning their heads.

Rhinoceros

Rhinoceroses are some of the largest land animals in the world. They can weigh up to 2,300 kg (5,070 pounds) and stand over 6 feet (1.8 metres) tall.

The name rhinoceros means 'nose horn' and its often shortened to rhino The horn is made of keratin, the same material as human hair and nails.

A group of Rhinoceros is called a crash. They like to spend their time bathing in mud baths to keep cool.

Raccoon

Raccoons are found throughout North and Central America. They are known for their distinctive markings, including a black mask around their eyes and black bands around their tails.

Raccoons are intelligent animals and have been known to learn how to open trash cans, doors, and other objects in order to access food.

Raccoons are excellent climbers and are able to scale trees and buildings. They have special hands that allow them to grasp objects similar to humans.

Reindeer

Reindeer are the only deer species in which both males and females grow antlers. They shed and regrow their antlers eac year.

Reindeer have large, broad hooves that help them walk on snow and ice. along with a thick coat of fur that helps them stay warm.

Reindeer are known for their annual migration, which can cover thousands of miles as they travel between their summer and winter habitats.

102

Rat

Rats are able to remember complex layouts for up to several months, and can navigate mazes and other environments with ease.

Rats have incredibly sharp teeth and can gnaw through metal, concrete, and even cinder blocks.

Rats have been used in scientific research for over 150 years, and have been important in advancing our understanding of genetics, neuroscience, and disease.

Can you remember?

What are baby rabbits called?

Answer

Kits

Shark

The great white shark is the largest predatory fish in the world, able to grow up to 20 feet (6 metres) in length and weighing over 2,200kg (5,000 pounds).

Sharks continually shed their teeth. Some shed approximately 35,000 teeth in a lifetime, replacing those that fall out.

Sharks have been around for over 400 million years, making them older than dinosaurs. They can grow very old and migrate thousands of miles each year.

Squirrel

There are over 200 species of squirrels, found all over the world, except in Australia and Antarctica.

Squirrels have four toes on their front feet and *five* on their back feet, which helps them grip tree branches and climb easily..

The biggest squirrel is the Indian giant squirrel, which can grow up to 39 inches (1 metre) long. The smallest is the tiny African pygmy squirrel which is 2.8-5 inches (7-13cm).

Sloth

Sloths are known for being slow-moving animals. They move so slowly that algae can grow on their fur, providing them with a natural camouflage in the trees.

Sloths are able to rotate their heads up to 270 degrees, which allows them to see behind them without moving their bodies.

Sloths can move up to three times faster when they swim and hold their breath for up to 40 minutes!

Seahorse

Seahorses are fish that are found in shallow, tropical waters. They have a unique body shape, with a long snout, small mouth, and tail that can grab things.

They are one of the only animals on earth where the male gets pregnant and gives birth to the young.

They are very good at hiding, and their unique shape and ability to change colour allows them to blend in with the plants and animals in their environment.

Seal

Seals are really good swimmers and can hold their breath for up to 2 hours while diving. They can reach depths of 1000 feet (300 metres).

Male seals are called bulls, females are called cows and babies are called pups. They have a thick layer of fat called blubber under their skin to keep them warm in icy water.

There are over 30 different species of seals, including fur seals, sea lions, and elephant seals. They are carnivores and primarily feed on fish, squid, and krill.

Can you remember?

How many species of squirrels are there?

Answer
Over 200

Tiger

Tigers are the largest cats in the world, with some species weighing over 226 kg (500 pounds). They have powerful jaws and can bite through bones and thick hides.

Tigers have excellent night vision and can see six times better than humans in the dark, which makes them great hunters.

A tiger's roar can be heard up to 2 miles away, making it one of the loudest animal sounds in the world.

Tasmanian devil

Tasmanian devils are small, carnivorous marsupials that are native to the island state of Tasmania, located off the coast of Australia.

Tasmanian devils have powerful jaws and can bite through bones. They have one of the strongest bite forces in the animal kingdom.

Tasmanian devils are named after the sound of their loud ferocious growl, which can be heard up to a mile away.

Turtle

There are over 300 species of turtles. Some can *live* for over 100 years, with the oldest recorded turtle living to be 188 years old.

Sea turtles can swim up to 35 mph and can hold their breath for up to 5 hours. They have a strong sense of smell and use it to locate food and navigate.

Turtles have a hard shell that protects them from predators. It is made up of about 50 bones fused together. Some can retract their head and limbs into their shell for added protection.

Toucan

Toucans are brightly coloured birds native to Central and South America, known for their large and distinctive beaks.

Toucans have zygodactyl feet, which means that they have two toes pointing forward and two toes pointing backward, which helps them to grip branches and climb trees.

They have a specially designed tongue that is long and narrow, which they use to catch insects and to drink nectar from flowers.

114

Tarantula

The Goliath birdeater tarantula, found in South America, is the largest spider in the world by mass, with some weighing over 170 grams (6 ounces).

Tarantulas are often kept as pets by enthusiasts and can be trained to recognise their owners and even be hand-fed. They can *live* for up to 30 years.

Tarantulas are known for their impressive ability to regenerate lost limbs, a trait shared by many spiders.

Can you remember?

How did Tasmanian devils get their name?

Answer
From their loud growl

Uakari

Uakaris are a type of monkey that live in the Amazon rainforest of South America. They are known for their distinctive red faces.

Uakaris are able to jump long distances between trees, and can make leaps of up to 30 feet in a single bound.

They have a large brain relative to their body size, and are considered to be one of the most intelligent of the New World monkeys.

Urial

Urial are a wild sheep with long legs and relatively small horns, native to central Asia.

Males have large, curved horns that can grow up to 4 feet (1.2 metres) in length, while females have smaller, straighter horns.

They are well adapted to the rugged, mountainous terrain of their habitat and are able to climb steep slopes and navigate rocky terrain with ease.

Unicorn

Unicorns are often associated with rainbows, and in some legends, it was believed that their horns could create rainbows.

The national animal of Scotland is the unicorn, which is depicted as a white horse with a golden horn.

Some cultures believe that seeing a unicorn in a dream is a sign of good luck and good fortune.

Can you remember?

where do ukaris live?

Virginia opossum

The Virginia opossum is the only marsupial found in North America. They have a lifespan of around 2-4 years in the wild.

Opossums have a unique immune system that allows them to resist the venom of certain snakes and spiders.

Virginia opossums have a unique defence mechanism known as "playing possum" where they fake death by rolling onto their side, becoming limp, and releasing a foul-smelling liquid.

Vole

Voles are small rodents that are often mistaken for mice. They have round ears, short tails, and stocky bodies. There are around 155 species.

Voles are known for their ability to create complex burrow systems underground. These burrows serve as shelter from predators and provide access to food sources.

Voles are able to swim and are known to use streams and other waterways to travel between habitats.

Vulture

Some species of vultures have a wingspan of up to 10 feet (3 metres), making them some of the largest birds in the world.

Vultures are scavenging birds that feed on the carcasses of dead animals. They are often seen circling high in the sky looking for food.

Vultures have a relatively long lifespan compared to other birds, with some species living up to 30 years in the wild.

Can you remember?

Where can you find Virginia opossum?

Answer
North America

Wolf

Wolves use body language and vocalisations to communicate with each other. Their howl can be heard from up to 6 miles away.

Wolves have a special adaptation in their paws that allows them to walk on snow without sinking in.

Wolves can run for long distances without getting tired, and they can keep up their speed for hours.

Wombat

Wombats are native to Australia and are marsupials, meaning they carry their young in a pouch like kangaroos and wallabies.

Wombats have been known to dig burrows up to 100 feet (30 metres) long and 10 feet (3 metres) deep.

Wombats are very strong and have been known to knock over gates and fences with ease. They can live for up to 15 years in the wild.

Warthog

Warthogs are a type of wild pig found in Africa. They are known for their distinctive appearance, with two pairs of tusks.

Their sharp tusks are not only used for defence, but also for digging up food and digging burrows for shelter.

Warthogs have a tough hide that is good at defending against the teeth and claws of predators.

Walrus

Walruses are large marine mammals that live in the Arctic Ocean and surrounding seas. They are known for their long tusks.

Their thick, wrinkled skin helps to insulate them from the cold. They can weigh up to 1.5 tons and grow to be up to 11 feet long (3.3m).

Walruses are able to hold their breath for up to 30 minutes and can dive to depths of up to 300 feet (91m). They can swim up to speeds of 21 miles per hour.

Woodpecker

There are over 180 different species of woodpeckers found worldwide, with a variety of sizes and colours.

Woodpeckers have a unique adaptation in their neck that allows them to rapidly move their head back and forth while pecking.

Woodpeckers use their long, sticky tongues to capture insects hiding inside wood or under bark.

Can you remember?

where are wombats native to?

<u>Answer</u>

Australia

Xantus

Xantus's Hummingbird is named after a Hungarian naturalist, John Xantus de Vesey, who collected the first specimen in 1859.

Xantus hummingbirds are able to fly backwards, hover in place, and fly upside down.

It is one of the few species of hummingbirds that has a green back and a rusty-coloured belly. Males have a vibrant pink throat patch, which they use to attract females.

Xenopus

Xenopus frogs are also known as "African clawed frogs" because they have webbed feet with small claws.

Xenopus are used in scientific research, particularly in genetics and developmental biology. They are able to regenerate certain body parts, such as their limbs and eyes.

Xenopus have special ears that allow them to hear low-frequency sounds, such as the calls of their predators. They produce a toxic mucus when threatened.

Xenops

Xenops are small, brown birds found in Central and South America.

They have a distinctive upward-curved bill, which they use to pry insects from tree bark.

They have a special toe arrangement that allows them to cling to vertical surfaces. They have a unique habit of roosting upside down under branches.

Can you remember?

what is another name
for the xenopus frog?

Answer
African clawed frog

Yacare caiman

The Yacare caiman is a species of caiman that is found in the wetlands of South America, particularly in the Pantanal region of Brazil.

Yacare caimans can grow up to 6.5 feet (2 metres) in length, with males being slightly larger than females.

Yacare caimans have a long, powerful tail that they use to propel themselves through the water, and strong jaws that they use to catch and hold their prey.

Yak

Yaks are a type of cattle that *live in the* Himalayan region of central Asia, including Tibet, Nepal, and Bhutan.

Yaks are well-adapted to *living in high-altitude* environments, with thick, shaggy fur that keeps them warm in cold temperatures.

The wild yak is the largest native animal of the Himalayan region, with males weighing up to 1,000kg (2,200 pounds). They are known for their strength and are used by people for transportation.

Yeti crab

Yeti crabs are a type of deep-sea crab that was discovered in 2005 near hydrothermal vents in the South Pacific Ocean.

Yeti crabs have a hairy appearance on their bodies and claws, which give them a resemblance to the mythical yeti creature.

They are only found in the deep sea, at depths of around 7,000 feet (2,100 metres) The hydrothermal vents that they call home are some of the most extreme environments on Earth.

Can you remember?

where would you find a Yacare caiman?

Answer
South America

Zorilla

Zorillas are sometimes called "stink badgers" because they are related to skunks and are known for their potent musky odor.

The musk produced by Zorillas is so strong that it can linger in an area for weeks or even months after the animal has left.

Zorillas are known for their bold and aggressive behaviour, and will often stand their ground and confront predators much larger than themselves.

Zebra

No two zebras have the same pattern of stripes, making each zebra's pattern unique and like a human fingerprint.

Zebras are able to sleep while standing up, with one eye open to keep watch for predators.

Zebras can run at speeds of up 40 miles per hour, making them one of the fastest land animals in the world.

Zigzag salamander

The Zigzag Salamander is a species of salamander found in the eastern United States. It gets its name from the zigzag pattern on its back.

The Zigzag Salamander is usually found in cool, damp forests near streams or other bodies of water.

The Zigzag Salamander is a small species, growing to a maximum length of around 6 inches (15 cm).

Can you remember?

What other name do
Zorillas have?

Answer
Stink badgers

Thank you for reading along with me animal fanatics! I hope you have learned some fantastic facts about all of my animal friends to share with your friends, family and anyone who will listen.

If you enjoyed this book <u>please leave a positive review</u> and keep an eye out for the other books in the fantastic facts series.

Printed in Great Britain
by Amazon

25315225R00082